A CUP OF TEA WITH A SIDE OF CANDY AND LEMONS. SAYINGS, EXPERIENCES, HEARTACHE'S AND HOW I'VE MANAGED TO STAY FOCUSED THROUGH LIFE.

A Cup Of Tea With A Side Of Candy And Lemons. Sayings, Experiences, Heartache's And How I've Managed To Stay Focused Through Life.

AS TOLD BY STACEY OAKLEY

Bruce Oakley Contributor

Tools I

Contents

DEDICATION

I must give all Glory to God first!
To My Husband Bruce, What an inspiration and
UNBELEIVABLE GIFT, you have been to me and
my baggage! Because of you, I've gained
UNSPEAKABLE, Love, Confidence and renewed
self worth. I NEVER thought I would ever be
soo BLESSED to have You. My Angels
Ronie, Seaun, John, Carter(My BooBoo Cat)
Zayiden and Tator.
I Love You.

R.I.H MOM.
R.I.H DADDY.
Thanks Shervonne! You Rock(you almost got
us kicked out of my
Daughters Gated Community! You're such a
BEAUTIFUL spirit!

Northside!

Learn How To Communicate

No matter where you live or what you do or do not have, The right communication for change is kcy!

Like the 1'st chapter says, Pour your own cup.

FOLKS! If you're not to updated about vocabulary words, this is the advise you should write down. There are soo many meanings to words. You should know your words and what they mean.! Pick up a dictionary. Dem, Dey and Dos will not be in there? Teach yourselves grammer as well as diction.

I ALWAYS, got criticized about how I spoke(at least by the black community)I know how to use my grammer and diction. I was accused of trying to speak like another race because of my grammer and how to pronounce my words. I was real stiff on my children about this. I never talked baby talk to them. I would always correct them when they would pronounce words wrong. Teach yourselves! Do Not sit back and rely on somone else.

No matter who you are, do not think you have to live in a welfare state of mind!

Abuse Is Never Ok!

LISTEN FOLKS! Love should never hurt.

If you're in a relationship and you feel so much as a mosquito bite and your partner does noting to soothe it , RUUUN!

See folks, Allow me to enlighten you about some of the mental, physical, financial and personal abuse I've suffered at the hands of cowards whom I thought loved me,

This first COWARD, would hold and squeeze the underside of my chin for at least 20 minutes at a time(with his thumb and first finger) This way nobody could tell what he had done to me. He would ALWAYS, ensure that when he struck me it would be in places on my body that could not be detected. This PUNK, knocked my front teeth to the back of my mouth and I lied to everyone and said I slipped on ice. Have you ever been stalked by your abuser? What if you have a twin who's feeding your stalker your every move knowing her friend is screwing your stalker? This same person used to hide outside of my workplace and wait for me to leave work. He stopped that shit once a man named Marlon Burns whipped his ass. I Have not one ounce of doubt that this sick mother fucker is STILL doing these types of things to women. I hope his significant other is aware of his 5th child. Or of the fact that her best friend knows he's sleeping with one of her friends?

Hmmmm. The apple never falls far from the tree! There's a story about it. A person has a tendency to repeat things they have seen but I'm not going to go there!

All I have to say about the next Coward is Sit Your Dumb, Funky, 9 toe having ass down some Damn where! Baker University gave you your degree because they felt sorry for your dumb ass! I'm the one who filled out and submitted information regarding the job you've been at and have now. Let us all pray for that little soul you beat out of me in May of 2012 when I was five months pregnant. Be sure to let everyone know how you spit on me as you pushed me down. You're a monster!

I pray for your soul.

Forgive them father, for they know not what the do.

If you or someone you know is in an abusive situation PLEASE, contact

The National Domestic Abuse Hotline At 800-799-7233

Chapter One

Pour Your Own Damn Cup!

This one is DEEP! I know some folks will relate to this. I had a couple of Ladies say this to me when I was younger. The first was a lady that went by the name of Mrs. Juanita.

Mrs Juanita was sharp as a tack! She would wait for the city bus or walk to work everyday. She was in her 70's at the time. Mrs Juanita had holes in her shoes. The holes did not deter her from going to work every-day! Looking back there are times I've felt bad about joining in with the rest of the neighborhood kids and teasing her about her holey shoes.

It was not until I encountered Mrs. Jaunita sitting on the brick wall one day waiting for the city bus. I was fortunate enough to spend a little time with her and listen.

Mrs Juanita explained to me " You must be your own self. Nobody is going to give you nothing in this life. You can't live off of what other folks think about you! Do not allow anyone to tell you how much you should have in your cup. Don't judge. These shoes of mine are not yours.

Chapter Two

Friends. How Many Of Us Have Them?

Unfortunately I've had to learn the hard way about friends. Everyone is NOT, your friend. I've always been the type to try trust. Trust has cost me a lot! A WHOLE LOT! Even family can fall into the category of everyone is not your friend. See folks, there really are people you come across in life who would love to steel your joy, see you fail.

This I Know. Read about the Seven, Deadly Sins!

My Mother always tried to in still in her girls, Family First and staying close.

Little did I know this would come back and bite me. You see, once I left my home town, I felt I was treated differently and looked at like I thought I was better than where I came from. In my opinion, this or that was an effect of someone who was uninformed about life outside of the surpressing town I lived in at the time.

After the death of my Mother and my Daddy I was smacked in the face with the reality of what love really meant.

All the while I thought I was trying to show how I had defeated the impoverished place I was raised in and was also proud of. I came to the realization that I was being looked at in a bad way by my sister's, I realized that my mother was the person keeping them from vocally, telling me what they **REALLY**, thought about me. I'm a twin. Yep we're 3 minutes apart. Question? How do forgive your twin when you know you were betrayed by the person who was 3 minutes born after you? How do you trust in a sibling who tout's God but does the opposite? How do you look up to a sister whom claims to be the big sister but has not a clue about life? I was faced with the fact that material things meant more to my siblings than me? I never talked about the expense of going back and forth from Kansas to Indiana. We would have done it 5,00000000 more times for my mother. Nobody offered a place to stay, cooked us a meal NOTHING!

I've since had to seriously, forgive, trust and know Through Christ All Things Are Possible.

What about that friend who's been married since the creation of time but is cheating on his or her spouse and you know about it? I find myself saying the Serinity Prayer sometimes. WOW, is all I've got for this one!

For everyone who has affected my life in any way, I say Thank You.

I'm wiser. I smile more. I'm in love with my Husband. I'm in need of nothing.

Chapter Three

Just a few sayings I've heard.

(These are from my mother first)

Bit$H please, F'um and feed them beans, You can get a wet A$# anywhere. I'm going to Cold Cock that ass. Whatchu doing BI^%#? Now keep this to yourself. It's just mom.

Kjiss my P^%Y. Let me tell you about this dumb B*&$H! Don't make me cuss you out! Give me noise! Where's Bruce's Black Ass At?

Random things I've heard.

I wouldn't give you the gum off of the bottom of my shoe- I'd chew it first before giving it to you! River Rat, Dirty Whore, Bed Bug Bitch! WOW, OMG, Game recognizes's game and bullshit recognizes bullshit.

You're stupid. Shut up, UnUhhhh, What is Felot Mengion? OMG! Bet that! I Love You. You are soo dumb, Anyway!

Chapter Four

Break your mold people. You can do anything you dream of. Where you live at doesn't mean you can't be successful. Learn how to rise above the stereo types. There's a lot from the hood who have done this.

Educate yourselves, Know your rights and local laws.

Be well my friends.

Chapter Five

There's more to come!

Never Forget Where You Came From

I have not 1 doubt I'm not the only person who grew up without.

the one thing I never was without, was love. No matter the circumstances love was sometimes always presented. There are few things I would change regarding the way and where I was raised.

I'm not sure as to why the Northside of most cities is looked at as a negitave side of town? My experience growing up on the Northside Of Richomond In, was that people from the Southside and Westide would venture to the Northside and do dirt and flee? Leaving the Northside of town to blame.

Although I've been long removed from the Northside of Richmond In, I always ride through when I visit. I always looked forward to going to look at what was the water fall. Getting my pipe(spring water)water from Glenn Miller Park. The fresh springs are still there. Clara's pizza is always a must.

To me, when I visit my home town it seems suppressed? It feels slow to me.

All I have left there are memories. Buemes grocery store. Millers milk house. The power house. Hooks drug store. Mr. Pugh. Banana nose. The bait shop. Townsend Community Center. Neighborhood green tanks. Nicholson School Yard. JoAnn's Bakery. Veaches toy store with the Birthday castle. Looking back on where I lived, I now realize, we lived in what today, would've been labeled A Food Dessert. I'm grateful for where I came from and what I learned. Northside will ALWAYS, run deep in my soul.